Fairey-isms

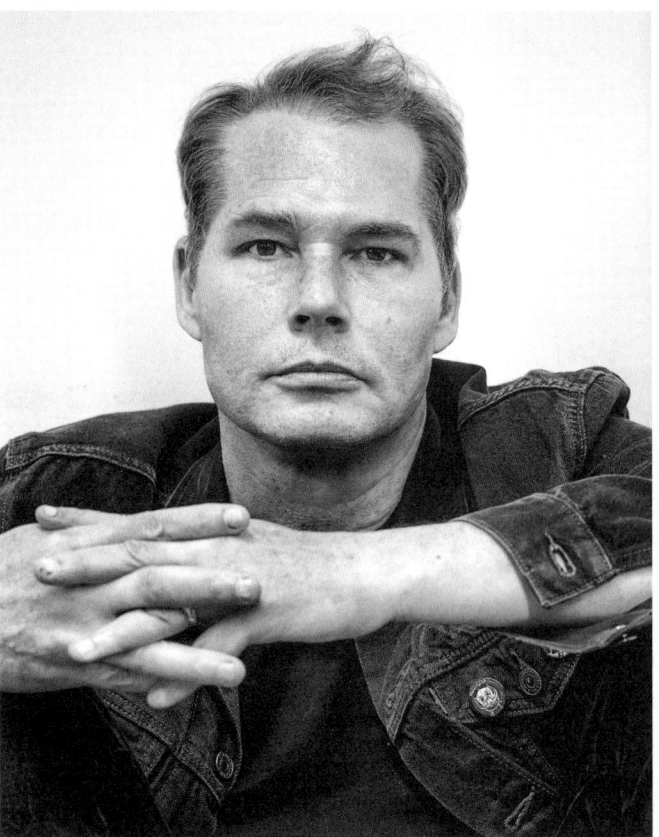

Fairey-isms

Shepard Fairey

Edited by Larry Warsh

PRINCETON UNIVERSITY PRESS
Princeton and Oxford

in association with
No More Rulers

Princeton University Press is committed to the protection of
copyright and the intellectual property our authors entrust to us.
Copyright promotes the progress and integrity of knowledge created
by humans. Thank you for supporting free speech and the global
exchange of ideas by purchasing an authorized edition of this
book. If you wish to reproduce or distribute any part of it in
any form, please obtain permission.

Requests for permission to reproduce material from this work
should be sent to permissions@press.princeton.edu

Published by Princeton University Press,
41 William Street, Princeton, New Jersey 08540

In the United Kingdom: Princeton University Press,
99 Banbury Road, Oxford OX2 6JX
press.princeton.edu
in association with
No More Rulers
nomorerulers.com
ISMs is a trademark of No More Rulers, Inc.

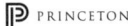 PRINCETON   ~~NO MORE RULERS~~ ®

All Rights Reserved
ISBN 9780691271415
Library of Congress Control Number: 2024944434
British Library Cataloging-in-Publication Data is available

This book has been composed in Johanna MT
Printed in China
1 3 5 7 9 10 8 6 4 2

CONTENTS

INTRODUCTION vii

Art and Creativity 1

Inspirations and Influences 15

Approaches and Methods 31

Street Art 45

Communication and Propaganda 63

Effecting Change 81

Point of View 101

SOURCES 123

CHRONOLOGY 137

ACKNOWLEDGMENTS 150

INTRODUCTION

When I think of Shepard Fairey, "intelligent disrupter" is the term that comes to mind—an artist with a conscience and a true communicator of our time. In paintings, prints, posters, and a range of other mediums, Fairey gives us a fresh take on what it means to make art today, and to connect with audiences far beyond the usual museum and gallery system. For Fairey, the city is a canvas, and he is uniquely attuned to the visual conversations that take place every day on urban streets. Rethinking the meaning of "propaganda," Fairey demystifies images, turns them into language, and challenges us to think critically about the onslaught of messaging that envelops us every day. Based on the visual vocabulary of Chinese and Russian propaganda, his striking graphic style drives home a fundamental message: question everything.

Growing up in South Carolina, Fairey was inspired by punk, hip-hop, music, skateboarding, and graffiti—essential elements of contemporary international youth culture. He began by stenciling and screen printing his drawings onto T-shirts, skateboards, and stickers. From this came the iconic "Andre the Giant" sticker campaign. Initially aimed at making his reputation among his peers, the sticker quickly went viral. To date, this image—and its later version, the stylized face of Andre the Giant with the word "OBEY" in bold font capital letters—have seen more than a million copies worldwide.[1] In its impact, reach, and influence, Fairey's art is global.

Across his creative output, Fairey combines careful method with a direct point of view: he is inventive in his approaches and independent in mind and thought. His activism is aimed at improving the system, using what we might call "mainstream messaging." Sited in city streets, Fairey's art emphasizes the importance of public places. His wife, Amanda, and their children are important inspirations, and much of his creative effort supports causes that will help secure a livable future for them and for everyone. Those causes include environmental conservation, human rights, and civic engagement—most famously, the unofficial "Hope" campaign poster he created for Barack Obama in 2008.

But Fairey's approach to political art is inviting rather than instructive. He leaves room for viewers to make up their own minds. His goal is to start the conversation, not finish it. Charitable and caring, active and involved, he draws energy from the street and intensifies it with his own contributions. In our daily lives, he makes us stop and think—and invites us to appreciate not only his art but the walls it's pasted on. Fairey makes street art stand tall.

Gathered from interviews, articles, and Fairey's own writings, the quotations in this book explore the inner workings of a dynamic artist. From his early influences and approaches to artmaking to his thoughts on social justice and community involvement, *Fairey-isms* aims to give readers an expanded understanding of this icon of contemporary street art.

At this moment, the home page of Fairey's website proudly proclaims: "Manufacturing Quality Dissent Since 1989."[2] He is dedicated to making art for the people—and for the future. It is art for a purpose—art for change.

LARRY WARSH

1 "Obey Giant—Andre The Giant Face (Black & White) Description," Artstor, https://library.artstor.org/# /public/29732136.
2 See https://obeygiant.com/.

Art and Creativity

I consider myself a populist artist. I want to reach people through as many different platforms as possible. (28)

———

I want to demystify art. (11)

———

When I say art, I'm talking about the design of the next iPhone, video game, a movie, a book cover, an album cover.
Art is everywhere. (71)

———

I never set out to be a groundbreaking artist,
in the sense of doing something that's never
been done before. I set out to make stuff that
communicated quickly and effectively, playing
off of advertising, pop art, and pop culture.

(15)

———

It's important for art to have a point of view.

(34)

———

Art should work conceptually,
not just aesthetically. (11)

———

They say a picture is worth a thousand words, but how do you condense a thousand words into a picture? (52)

Visual problem solving and illustration are very good therapy for me. I get to incorporate my ideas, my sense of humor, my pop culture nostalgia, my antagonism, and my conception of beautiful and powerful aesthetics into my art. (24)

Even with challenging subject matters I can find joy and therapy in trying to confront them. Art, making pictures, is always joyful. (65)

Not all of my pieces are activist or politically oriented in an overt way. Waves and the ocean have several symbolic elements I'm drawn to, and I find the water's surface beautiful and hypnotic. When I make art of waves, I'm hoping the viewer will think about things like the power of nature, rising sea levels, and the valuable but delicate ecosystems within the ocean. (48)

————

I'm interested in making things that are powerful, and ignoring these sort of categories and boundaries that other people put up. (16)

————

What I'm interested in is democratizing art, making people feel like they can participate, not just be spectators, and feel like it's not only a game rigged for the privileged. (57)

———

My activism is part of what I think my strongest talent is, which is making images coupled with a point of view. (64)

———

Art needs to hit people on a visual level that they enjoy and intuitively they're going to respond to when they see it. (39)

———

[Art] can crystallize information in a way that nothing else can. (52)

———

Art is incredibly important, because what does the United States export? Culture. That's our biggest export. It's absolutely foolish to de-emphasize it. (71)

———

Art and commerce need each other, though they often don't understand each other. (52)

———

The arts keep people from being robots. You build self-esteem through creativity. You learn problem-solving skills. It's adaptive. (73)

———

Art is all about problem solving. (58)

———

Creative people adapt better. (73)

———

What I hope people take away from my image,
if they care to look at my history, is that an
artist can be multidimensional, they can fuse a
lot of different things they care about into
what they do every day. It's not necessary to
paint yourself into a corner with categories.

(69)

———

For most people becoming a painter, a fine
artist, is very unrealistic. There's a very, very
small percentage of people who can pull
that off as a career. (69)

———

I try to just take a deep breath and do my thing one day at a time. I think my instincts have served me pretty well. (67)

———

There's accessibility and then desirability. If people like the concept of what I'm doing and also visually it's compelling enough to them to want to spread it, then they also have to be able to easily access it. The internet really helps that. (46)

———

Being shown in galleries has catalyzed an evolution in my work and things are coming out that I didn't notice before because I'm spending more time with my pieces. (49)

———

When it comes to the tortoise and the hare,
I'm with the tortoise. (66)

––––––––

I love the concept in fine art of making a
masterpiece, something that will endure. But I
also understand how short the attention span
of most consumers is and that you really need
to work with the metabolism of consumer
culture, a lot of times, to make something
relevant within the zeitgeist. (69)

––––––––

The way I make art—the way a lot of people make art—is as an extension of language and communication, where references are incredibly important. It's about making a work that is inspired by something preexisting but changes it to have a new value and meaning that doesn't in any way take away from the original—and, in fact, might provide the original with a second life or a new audience. (62)

I enjoy curating because it's an opportunity to tell a story and highlight art and people I think are deserving. ... This all impacts my work in the form of inspiration and connection, which is predominantly what art is about anyway. (48)

———

Street art is one way to reach people, and I appreciate its accessibility and confrontational nature, but I also like to make paintings that have a more sophisticated and nuanced surface that can be appreciated as art objects and digested over time unlike street art that usually is viewed for a short amount of time and is almost always temporary. (56)

———

I love that art on the street has its own life,
evolves and develops on its own. It's a sort
of beautiful chaos. (49)

———

I do think that graffiti street art is not
appropriate everywhere, and I feel that my
approach is to try to find the most appropriate
places where the art can be integrated. (46)

———

A lot of work on the street doesn't last,
so I aim for maximum impact within a
potentially short life span. (21)

I really enjoyed the freedom of anonymity I had for years, because I felt people interpreted my art without the added complication of throwing what I look like or other aspects of my personality into the equation. (24)

———

My do-it-yourself mentality is the same as it has always been, I just have more resources and more opportunities now. (13)

———

It's always the next one. The next one's gonna be the best. (19)

———

Inspirations and Influences

I've drawn and painted my whole life—my goal was to make art by any means necessary. (14)

———

My parents are very disciplined, and they did teach me, as much as I rebelled, that you don't let people down by not delivering on your word. (7)

———

Living in Charleston did influence my artistic direction in a number of ways. I think everyone is impacted by their environment. (13)

———

I grew up drawing and painting traditionally, but when I got into skateboarding and punk rock in 1984, I became interested in screen printing and stenciling to make homemade T-shirts and stickers. (31)

———

[Skateboarding] was the first thing I did that was fun, liberating, and creative in both the activity and the culture. (31)

———

Skateboarding changed my life. Punk rock changed my life. Everything I've been into since then, in terms of do-it-yourself culture, has really come from that. (43)

———

I think "punk" should really be defined as paving your own way creatively and by defying any sort of orthodoxy or commercial pressure. (24)

———

When I was young, my icons were the Santa Cruz Skateboards logo, the Black Flag logo, the anarchy symbol, and the peace sign. That's what I sort of understood as icons. Symbols that people could recognize, whether they were mainstream culture or subculture.

(72)

———

All the subcultures that I've ever been interested in, whether it was skateboarding, punk rock, hip-hop, or graffiti, all started off as if there are no rules. They were a clean slate. Do whatever you want. Be a rule breaker. Then they slowly develop an orthodoxy. (57)

———

My parents had expressed their dislike of anything skate or punk related and would provide no financial support for additions to my wardrobe in these categories. (4)

———

Nobody can tell you what real hip-hop is because real hip-hop broke the rules from the beginning. (16)

———

Street art gave me liberation from
hyper-analysis, and this freedom is something
I still enjoy today. (52)

———

Skateboarding definitely isn't as punk rock
as it used to be. (68)

———

When I am asked about my biggest influences,
my interrogator is often surprised to hear
"The Sex Pistols," "Black Flag," "Public
Enemy," generally expecting me to list
off visual artists. (3)

———

Music is something that I've been passionate about since I was a kid, but when I discovered punk rock and realized that music could have an attitude in its style but a specific point of view in its lyrics, I became even more interested in how it works as a way of shaping attitudes and culture. (56)

———

I came to punk rock through skateboarding. If you got into skateboarding you had to listen to The Clash, The Sex Pistols, The Dead Kennedys, Bad Brains, Black Flag, etc. (57)

———

I secretly liked Black Sabbath, Motorhead, and Metallica, but if you were punk rock you weren't allowed to be vocal about what were seen as the rival genres. But then ultimately good music is good music and I stood up for it. (67)

———

No matter how much I love art, or try to convince myself of its relevance in society, the fact remains that music is a lot cooler. (3)

———

The truth is, I always fell asleep during art history lectures in college, but I've never fallen asleep at a single concert. Am I the exception? I don't think so. (3)

———

Music provides a cultural ecosystem in and of itself. There's the actual music, the lyrics with their content and politics, the style and personalities of the bandmembers and the politics implicit in their lifestyles, and lastly, their art, album packaging and graphics. (3)

———

I love the accessibility of music; it is democratic in a way that most visual art is not. In fact, I emulate the music model in the ways that I disseminate my visual art. (56)

———

I've long been inspired by the various printing processes as an empowering means of creating and disseminating images. Printing plates are beautiful and powerful as objects and instruments. (48)

―――

There's something about print and having a tactile product that's so appealing. The virtual experience is never going to replace that. (66)

―――

I take inspiration from many art forms, from propaganda posters to album packaging, pop art like Barbara Kruger and Andy Warhol, and Jasper Johns and Robert Rauschenberg for the surfaces they created. (64)

―――

It pisses me off when people lose the ability to acknowledge or celebrate the people who inspired and influenced them. Learning is based on direct and indirect apprenticeship, but people like to act like they formed their ideas and themselves in the wilderness. (24)

I owe my red, black, and white color palette to Russian Constructivism and Barbara Kruger.
(74)

Barbara Kruger was a huge inspiration for me and I consider her a hero. (6)

Kruger has made a tremendous impact in several key areas of contemporary art: graphic design and appropriation, public address, and political content. (74)

———

Her style seemed to say, "This is art with political intent." (7)

———

Warhol was a huge role model for me in terms of expanding the role of art into broader culture and tackling subject matter that the art world considered mundane. (5)

———

I loved Futura because he worked with my favorite band The Clash and also designed T-shirts and other merchandise that fell loosely into the skateboard and streetwear worlds. (13)

———

TWIST [Barry McGee] was the first graffiti artist who I thought translated the energy of the street in the gallery environment in a way that succeeded at the highest level of installation of art and fine art. (13)

———

My approach definitely takes cues from [New York graffiti artists] Revs and Cost, as well as the worlds of advertising and propaganda. I learned from Revs and Cost that simplicity and ubiquity can cut through all the visual noise and urban clutter. (4)

I feel strongly that in the wake of Pop Art and the art world acceptance of the pop-culture vernacular it utilized, that fine art has increasingly been defined by intent rather than a traditional "art" aesthetic or particular technique like painting. (74)

I enjoy the challenge of making images that draw people into a conversation they might not otherwise have. (21)

———

We all know what it feels like to experience art that moves us, whether it's music, whether it's visual art, whether it's film, whether it's theater, whether it's stand-up comedy. (71)

———

The marriage of great art, great music, and great ideas is an incredibly powerful one. Hell, even two of those elements converging harmoniously yields something whose whole is more than the sum of its parts. (3)

———

I think everybody ends up being an
amalgamation of a lot of different influences
and I try to keep my eyes and mind open
to that stuff. (72)

———

I'm always looking at what's out there that
I think is strong. It could be brand new, but
it could be 500 years old. (72)

———

Approaches and Methods

Eyes open, mind open. (41)

———

The only reason I'm a decent artist is
because I experiment relentlessly. (72)

———

Perfection is never achievable and it's
always a work in progress. (47)

———

The cliché of the artist as a daydreamer
who works when inspiration strikes
does not fit me. (58)

———

My work is a combination of fun
and provocation. (1)

———

Repetition works, and stickers are a
perfect medium to demonstrate
this principle. (4)

———

Repetition works. (41)

———

The hardest part of maintaining independence
is that you are solely responsible for keeping
the lights on and keeping things moving. (54)

———

Finding evocative imagery and symbols that can translate complex ideas in relatable ways is far more challenging than making portraits. (40)

I've never put business before what I've wanted to say. (62)

Phenomenology attempts to enable people to see something right before their eyes but obscured, things so taken for granted that they are muted by abstract observation. I've always kept this fundamental idea at the core of all the work I do through street art, clothing, and fine art. These ideals are at the center of my creative practice. (50)

I try to make my clothing line an entry
point for discovering the substance of
the rest of my work. (43)

———

I don't think that fashion and integrity are
mutually exclusive. (43)

———

I've always thought of a T-shirt as a utilitarian,
unintimidating canvas. (1)

———

For me, fashion alone is elitist and boring. (1)

———

As my work's embraced by the mainstream,
here and there I'm using my ability to
infiltrate [the] mainstream to share
challenging messages with a broader
audience. I'm not pandering to the lowest
common denominator to find a
wider audience. (12)

———

Every time I make a piece, I'm thinking
of the best balance of saying what I want to
say in my style but also making sure
that it's relatable. (51)

———

I always err in favor of freedom of expression with the sole exception of exact, duplicate bootlegs. (24)

———

Though my art may make some people uncomfortable, I've always felt that provocation stimulating debate is much more desirable than ignoring sensitive issues to avoid hurting anyone's feelings. (2)

———

If I make an image that isn't visually striking then it doesn't matter how great the content of the idea is. (18)

———

For me it's important to be as engaging as possible and [large] scale is more confrontational. When someone does something larger, the viewer thinks it must be more important, and even if you make stickers with the same image, it will never have the same impact. (18)

I love the superficial as much as the next person, but I also like to weave in substance. (40)

I don't do anything without thinking it through. (19)

My inclusion of decorative elements may soften [works] visually, but upon further inspection actually intensifies the cautionary message in the works, because I've woven elements of the villains into the decorative elements in a way that is analogous to how they whitewash their insinuation and manipulation in our actual lives. (58)

———

It's extremely important for the work, whether it's in a gallery or a museum, to reflect the spirit of what I do on the street. So I create the work using the same methods—the screen printings, stenciling, collage—that I use for the street work. (46)

———

I love layering and the charm of organic deconstruction mixed with very graphic focal points. The layered surfaces of my works have a relationship to city walls caked with posters and paint. I like the implication that the layers in a piece reflect a history that led to that point. (64)

———

I've always liked the tension between spontaneous chaos and very resolved geometry. (44)

———

I'll press a sheet up onto a wall and the brick texture will seep through. This now becomes an added natural component to the piece. You can't recreate that in a gallery! (49)

As I'm illustrating, I'm trying to emphasize the elements that give the image its essence and remove everything that's superfluous. (45)

[The Obama "Hope" poster] was different from most political art in that it was a graphic image that was unique enough to stand out from what had come before it, but it was also tame enough to not scare people away. (5)

I'm always trying to make my work accessible
by delivering it through many platforms,
including public art, T-shirts, stickers, and
prints, as well as more expensive paintings.

(58)

———

I employ a Robin Hood approach,
if you will. I take the money that I make
from the commercial jobs and then I
support our gallery that we run in Los
Angeles, supplemental projects and various
other creative endeavors—charity projects,
pro bono work that I wouldn't be able
to do without that income. (46)

———

When I was younger, I bought into the typical black-and-white, us-versus-them simplification: provocation and silliness can't mix, a job has to be drudgery, passion is reserved for nights and weekends, and art can't be pure if it has a commercial facet. All that began to seem less valid as every small accomplishment with Obey Giant made it seem increasingly possible to do things my way. (38)

———

With the rapid pace of our culture, I don't think I can effectively reach a broad audience, and do projects with a high level of quality, unless I'm willing to collaborate and delegate. (58)

———

Collaboration forces you to step outside your comfort zone and formulas to find a solution that's harmonious with your own needs and the needs of your collaborator. Sometimes something really special happens when you bounce ideas off of someone. (58)

———

Some things that are great can take an hour, and some things that are great take weeks, months. (72)

———

I feel that it's important to use art as a tool of persuasion responsibly. Advertising uses the same techniques, not always for things that I think are good for people. (40)

———

Street Art

I don't want people to only experience my art in the safe, tame confines of the gallery, which is why I put my art up illegally in the streets. (3)

———

Everything that has happened for me as an artist has been a result of my willingness to take risks and put art on the streets in accessible places. (13)

———

True graffiti, to me, is just putting work you want out on the street for everyone to see without compromise. (1)

———

The excitement of the street will always beat
the excitement of a gallery show. (52)

———

Every opportunity I have stems from being a
risk-taker. To other people it's vandalism, and
it makes them feel like the fake structures they
cling to are eroding, and they're terrified.
I'm not that way. I love it. (37)

———

Street art has always been a way to, on a
shoestring budget, make an impact and
find a voice. (35)

———

Graffiti can never become too mainstream
because it is an activity, not a style. (1)

———

Every bit of graffiti is an act of self-expression
and self-empowerment. (19)

———

I was arrested in Denver during the
Democratic Convention [in 2008]. While
every vendor on every corner was selling my
Obama image, I was being arrested. (45)

———

[New York] is the birthplace of graffiti, and most people walk, so they actually have an opportunity to notice not only the big pieces of public art but even small things like a stencil or a sticker. (13)

———

Stickers were evidence that I wasn't living in a total void. (4)

———

Street art has to stand out from the static and contend with the metabolism of the city. (33)

———

One of the things that's been so exciting about street art is that it's in the public, people see it, it makes an impact, but it's also so ephemeral.
(11)

Street art is challenged or even augmented by its surroundings. … It's extremely important that the art can compete with all the other elements that surround it. The gallery can never replicate that. (52)

Murals change the landscape of a city and start conversations that wouldn't happen otherwise.
(31)

Art has the power to be visually appealing
and connect emotionally, but also create
a conversation and stimulate an
intellectual analysis. (10)

———

Some people define graffiti as only spray
paint, but I've always looked at any art done
on the street without permission as graffiti.
(13)

———

My work is about democratizing art and
empowering myself and other artists to have a
direct relationship with an audience. (50)

———

[Street art is] one of the most democratic
outlets for art and it rewards people with
talent and courage as opposed to more
elitist forums that reward connections
and resources. (17)

If art can crystallize a complex idea
in a relatable way, it can create important
conversations. (40)

My opinion about street art is the same as free
speech: I'd rather hear or see the occasional
thing I was offended by than not have the
right to express myself in a way that others
might find offensive. (76)

Street art is political by nature, because it is an act of defiance: saying I'm a citizen that's paying my taxes, I deserve a little chunk of public space, it shouldn't just be reserved for people who can afford to put an ad in a space because they have a product to sell. (16)

———

With street art, there is this "medium is the message" principle, that it's an act of defiance and rebellious in nature and that politicizes it. But that doesn't mean a street artist should just assume that whatever they're doing is groundbreaking and political because it's on the street. (34)

———

I'm always aware that my work on the street is ephemeral. It may last two weeks or two years; it will disintegrate or be covered. I've learned to enjoy the process. (20)

———

I enjoy the challenge of every mural as I'm doing it. They all have their idiosyncrasies. (58)

———

Everything gets messed with. It's just the nature of street art. You can't be too precious about it. (32)

———

On the street, people aren't bashful.
They will say if they like something or
if they think it sucks. (62)

———

To some people street art is vandalism, to
others it's gentrification, and either of those
could be considered more legit than the other
depending on your perspective. (14)

———

The argument that most lawmakers make
about graffiti is that it's illegal because it's an
eyesore, but you could easily argue that a
lot of advertising is an eyesore. (15)

———

Some of the street artists are anonymous
because they don't want to get in trouble;
others are anonymous because it's better for
their image. It's a much better selling point.

(51)

———

The Andre stickers started as a joke,
but I became obsessed with sticking them
everywhere both as a way to be mischievous
and also put something out into the world
anonymously but that I could
call my own. (4)

———

The beauty of the Andre image was that no one feels intimidated reacting to that image. Because wrestling is seen as the lowest brow culture. (11)

———

Andre, both in his life and in this image ["Andre the Giant Has a Posse" sticker], has this interesting balance between sinister and goofy, triumphant and tragic. (11)

———

Every sheet of stickers I printed felt like I was making the world a little smaller. (4)

———

Many stickers have been peeled down
by people who were annoyed by them,
considering them an eyesore and an act of
petty vandalism, which is ironic considering
the number of commercial graphic images
everyone in American society is
assaulted with daily. (8)

———

Clothing has always been very important to
me because it's very democratic, it's very
accessible, but murals and street art exist
where people live their lives. (42)

———

I think that galleries and museums have their
place, but they shouldn't be the only venues
for people to experience art. (70)

———

I always felt there's room for street art out there, and it is great that it is an alternative to all the advertising we're assaulted with. But I also think that there are a lot of different platforms for art that are valid platforms, whether they are galleries, museums, a T-shirt, an album package, a sticker, street art. People get into this, sort of, "genre fascism" that I think is holding them back and incredibly unhealthy, and I just refuse to be part of that.

(16)

―――

Museums and galleries legitimize art and secure its place in history. That being said, I believe the line is blurring now between art history and broader cultural history. (52)

―――

I'm grateful for walls. I think it is really, really incredibly, depressingly cynical to say, "Oh, well, someone gave a wall and it is part of a ruthless real estate scheme." There are ruthless schemes in abundance in the world. If something is supporting art, I tend to think that that person is better than 98 percent of the other people out there. (16)

———

My whole thing is that if there is a really great net positive in doing something that [means] you might have to engage with a company, but they facilitate a project that ends up really benefitting the kind of culture and art that you believe in, to me it was worth having to put a logo on a wall in the corner of an art show.

(63)

———

I'm too corporate for the street artist, and I'm too street for the corporate people. (45)

———

I look at all of the manifestations of my work as important, whether it's a T-shirt, a poster, street art, or fine art. (64)

———

Some in the art world have said that artists should be first-rate artists not second-rate social commentators. And I don't think the two should be mutually exclusive. (34)

———

The whole reason I got into street art in the
first place was because I wanted to bring art to
people rather than making people go to the
art. And the fact that some people don't like
the art being brought to them gives
me a lot of satisfaction. (75)

———

I think even if things were much more
utopian I would still find some things that
were worth making art about. (12)

———

Any message that's worth delivering can
be amplified with art. (9)

———

Communication
and Propaganda

I've always tried to use art as a tool of communication with all the means I had at my disposal. And whether that was putting posters up on a street, doing commercial projects, making T-shirts, making album covers, or getting involved in actual politics, these are all ways for me to share my ideas and try to make things happen the way I think they should happen and develop into the things I think they should develop into. (45)

———

My art is a tool of provocation, if not direct persuasion. (24)

———

Images in public that aren't advertising
make people curious. (46)

———

My work uses people, symbols, and people as
symbols to deconstruct how powerful visuals
and emotionally potent phrases can be used
to manipulate and indoctrinate. (2)

———

Everything has multiple agendas and the
viewer needs to look at both the immediate
read and the subtext. (69)

———

I want people to be suspicious of the visuals
they are inundated with and scrutinize things.
(24)

———

Investigate and deconstruct everything
because a person and the simplified symbol
they have become aren't always the
same thing. (2)

———

I have my frustrations with people that exploit
that psychology with the citizens, but I also
am frustrated with the citizens that
don't see through it. (61)

———

Figures are used symbolically for [a] group's agendas, simplifying them in a way which can never truly reflect the complexity of the individual. I use figures in my work who I feel are used and abused as symbols, but without telling the viewer how they should feel about them. I hope people that don't know the backgrounds of these leaders, radicals, pop icons, or movements will take the initiative to learn about their history. (2)

———

I called my work propaganda out of an understanding that there's an irony, because every piece of visual communication has an agenda. Any of it could be called propaganda. (19)

———

I have a conflicted relationship with oversimplified propaganda. ... I like my art to function as a gateway to a deeper conversation. (43)

———

Hopefully propaganda is not the basis of people's opinions, but a starting point that stimulates them to do their own research on a subject. (24)

———

Propaganda art is really powerful, and people fear it because they think that it has a sinister and manipulative agenda, but making art that has a point of view that's about correcting social ills and abuses of power, that's good propaganda. (11)

––––––

There is positive propaganda that is not about sinister indoctrination, but about making people aware of issues and making social commentary. (24)

––––––

A lot of the earlier posters that I did from around the mid-90s to around 2000 that were inspired by Russian constructivist propaganda and Cuban propaganda, Chinese propaganda, those images are really powerful in their design. Propaganda has a sinister connotation because it is so powerful [that] it has the ability to manipulate. (16)

———

[W]hat I was actually trying to do was riff off of a lot of that design, but in a way that was so obviously using the aesthetics of propaganda that it would encourage the viewer to question the role of propaganda. A lot of people didn't understand that irony in the work. (16)

———

I'm using the vehicle of fascist propaganda to parody commercial propaganda. (68)

———

The idea of propaganda and advertising being one and the same has been around for a while. (62)

———

People usually consider fascist propaganda as somewhat insidious, but they don't even question advertising, when they're being completely manipulated by advertising. (68)

———

De facto discrimination against the poor is
what billboards are. If you don't have money,
you can't rent a billboard. You can't get your
thing out. But that doesn't mean it's
any less important. (68)

———

Advertising is designed to make people
feel insecure. (53)

———

Most things are propaganda even if they
don't have a "propaganda" look. (24)

———

My work is a fusion of influences from
punk rock to propaganda posters—Cuban,
Soviet, and so on—but all produced to convey
something specific to the moment. (52)

———

A lot of my work is about getting people
to question obedience, question the control
of public space, question the nature of
propaganda, whether it is advertising
or anything else. I'm questioning
aspects of capitalism. (16)

———

I'm about working within capitalism even though I'm critiquing it and working within our two-party system of democracy but trying to make it better. (39)

———

I think it is important to remind people that there are people who benefit from the dynamics of capitalism and people that suffer under those same dynamics. (60)

———

I would like to see resources more evenly distributed so that people can have a decent quality of life. Call me a hippie. (70)

———

I use the word "Obey" in much of my art
as a form of reverse psychology. Though most
people wish they were independent, many
obediently follow the path of least resistance
and are uncomfortable with confronting
the word "Obey." (2)

———

The word "Obey" was just so glaringly
offensive to me, I always hated to be
told what to do. (11)

———

I consider the [OBEY] image the counterculture Big Brother. I'd like to think of it as a sign or symbol that people are watching Big Brother as well. (30)

———

[OBEY] was based on the idea that there are forces all around us that have agendas, but they are frequently unspoken. (62)

———

The irony is that I'm an image maker who's trying to get people to go deeper. And a lot of people only want to think about image. (61)

———

I wanted the [Obama] poster to be recognizable as my work, and to be appealing to a younger, apathetic audience, yet tame enough not to be seen as radical or offensive to the more mainstream political participants. (29)

———

There are narrow-minded people who criticize my art for Obama as "selling out" or "going mainstream." These people need to wake up and see that the only way to get the smaller problems fixed is to at least put someone in office who might be receptive to progressive ideas. (52)

———

Obama deserves all the credit for
being someone that just needed that
transmittable symbol to allow people to
express their enthusiasm for
him and share it. (47)

I refuse to endorse Obama simply because
he's a little more human and a little less
indifferent than the Republicans. (55)

I did make an effort to supplement my creation of the [Obama] poster by talking to the media and explaining in further detail why I supported Obama and what his policy positions were. It was supposed to be the first word of a sentence rather than the last. (66)

———

I've found the press tends to either portray me as a brainwashed Kool-Aid drinker who considers Obama the Messiah, or someone who has turned against him, when in reality I'm neither. (55)

———

To those who would criticize [the Obama poster] by calling it propaganda, I would say that it is not. Propaganda would be the last word in a conversation, and I am urging this to be the start of a conversation, maybe this is an option you haven't thought of. This is what a lot of my work is about. (7)

———

I'm not just trying to seduce people with an image, I'm trying to snap them out of a trance. (33)

———

Effecting Change

Anyone who isn't exasperated right now
isn't paying attention. (40)

———

The politics of our culture are about
consumption. No one cares about real
politics. It's all about who's got the money
and who's consuming what. (68)

———

I'm looking for people in government and a
system of government that creates the greatest
good for the greatest number of people,
democratically, without the influence of
corporations, or military contractors,
or other special interests. (55)

———

I really do believe that being patriotic is about questioning your government when it's not making you proud, but also supporting it when it is. (45)

———

One silver lining of the Trump years is that a lot of people who were pretty apathetic and complacent about politics have realized that it really matters who's in the White House. (65)

———

Bottom-up change only works when those in power don't think they can avoid the demands of the public. (55)

———

When greed and indifference is that status quo, it's time for conversation. (7)

———

I think that very little happens purely in the margins. You have to infiltrate the system. (19)

———

To stand for something takes courage. (27)

———

We only have so much time on the earth and I'm not going to waste a second of it. (27)

———

Every day should be Earth Day. (41)

———

Our system of democracy alienates some people, yet it is the system we have, and the only way to change it is through the system itself. You have to participate. (7)

———

Many people feel like spectators in our democracy because they don't feel qualified to weigh in and they don't think their vote counts for much anyway. Images that can generate a conversation empower people to feel confident about their right to voice their opinion, which leads to a more meaningful understanding of how they can participate in democracy and empower themselves. (40)

———

Democracy is for everyone, it's not just
for the powerful. (11)

Democracy doesn't work if people don't vote.
(61)

I think it's good for artists and everyone else
to weigh in politically. The people who are
greedy and will benefit from dominating the
political process certainly speak up, so
the rest of us should, too. (60)

I'm all for grassroots, but I'm all for also taking advantage of opportunities within the system and not just leaving the system to be run by people that you disagree with because you consider the system itself flawed. (47)

———

Social media activism is not what brings about change. It can be a component but you have to actually vote. You have to do things that actually sway politicians: call, petition, march in the street. (43)

———

If you don't like that vulnerable people are harmed by gentrification, vote for politicians that protect vulnerable people. (61)

———

Just go do it. People hold themselves back by
fears that they're not virtuosos. (26)

―――――

People are complacent and apathetic when
they're hopeless, and so hope leads to action.
It's also hard to be anti-hope. It's one of
those bulletproof things. (62)

―――――

We all need to be more engaged and educated
so we can distill truth from disinformation
and make the right choices as voters
and basic citizens. (55)

―――――

Cultural isolation is about preaching to the converted and never solves anything. (52)

———

I've always been one to "question authority," which just means don't always take things at their face value. Part of that means examining who controls the systems we work in and where their values lie. (49)

———

Democracy is failing because the influence of corporations means that the average person's needs are a much lower priority. (23)

———

Even an idealistic president will be handicapped by a congress that is looking out for its donors rather than its constituents. (23)

———

Anyone who says the dynamics of capitalism solve all problems hasn't watched the news lately. (40)

———

Even if it might not please everyone you do business with, I think standing up for what's right is admirable and more people should do it. (20)

———

I'm not an anarchist at all; I believe
in improving the system, not just
destroying things. (39)

———

Democracy is about a lot more than voting.
It unfortunately comes down to the average
person having to curb the influence of
deep-pocketed corporations with
perpetual vigilance. (65)

———

I don't have the patience for bureaucracy that
it would require to actually be in government,
but I'm glad to work with people who are
trying to make all the moves that take
things forward. (47)

———

I've been focusing on principles more than personalities, because the players change but if the dynamics of the system remain the same, even a candidate who I think has good ideas will be hindered. (21)

The players change but the problems stay the same. (14)

If you listen to a call-in sports show, the people know every single variable you can imagine, and if they only applied that same level of rigor to policy and the candidates that they choose, our political system would look very different. (71)

We live in a country that has largely glamorized the myth of the armed hero who protects the powerless and saves the day. (22)

———

Being complicit because it's the home team is nationalism, not patriotism. (25)

———

There are plenty of powerful people broadcasting loud messages of hate and division, so I think it's more than my right, but rather, my duty to make counterarguments as prominent as possible. (20)

———

I'm motivated to make art that I hope can make a difference and turn people out to vote. (5)

———

People compartmentalize art as escape and then reading the newspaper or watching the news or having a debate over social media as how you navigate social issues. I like that I think my art combines the two in a way that's fairly harmonious. (10)

———

Art impacts emotionally and study after
study has shown that people are driven
more by emotion than they are by intellectual
ideas, and that intellectual ideas coalesce
often around emotions. So there have been
people that use that in a really dangerous,
manipulative way for their own gain.
I would like to use those techniques in
a community-oriented, generous
spirit for everyone's benefit. (9)

———

People like to talk shit, but it's usually to
justify their own apathy. (15)

———

What's inexpensive for me is potentially out of reach, financially, for a lot of other artists … I want to advocate for other artists, not just myself. (43)

People say that my activist work is so generous. I say, "No it's not. I want to live in a better world—it's selfish!" (7)

I've had people ranging from anarchists to the president of the National Reserve Bank embrace my work, and I think the more diverse the audience is, the more potential for interesting dialogue there is. (30)

I'm going to keep making art and being a thorn in your side by protesting social ills and injustice, and doing it in a way that hopefully is creative and inspiring. (11)

———

I'm not trying to tell anybody how to think. I'm just hoping if they haven't considered something that they'll consider it. (47)

———

I just want to show that in a sea of very funded, cutthroat corporate competition, a grassroots campaign can make an impact with a little innovation and a lot of tenacity. (1)

———

Artists: give the companies credit for taking risks. Companies: give the artists money for taking risks. Everybody wins in this equation.

(36)

The racial justice protests, a lot of the art, all the murals, all the signs, the role that creativity can play is really being recognized by younger people and I couldn't be happier about that. (47)

I'm all about peace but I'm about justice too.

(39)

I'm always pulling for the underdog whether
I'm still the underdog or not. (1)

Anything is possible. (24)

Infiltrate the system and make it better
if you can. (6)

Disruption has many dimensions. (23)

If you need to take a stand and be abrasive,
wait until it counts and is absolutely necessary.

(7)

Always give people the benefit of the doubt, treat them well and make sure that you're respectful in your basic demeanor. (7)

———

Anger is only valuable if it fuels something meaningful. (19)

———

Empower yourself, question authority, question everything, do things your own way.
(11)

———

We're all responsible for shaping the future.
(42)

———

Point of View

I'm a populist. I want to be accessible. (51)

———

It's my philosophy to use my art to connect
with people in as many different areas of
culture as possible. (42)

———

There is no specific political affiliation behind
what I do, only the philosophy "question
everything." (2)

———

Pragmatism and experience have fueled
my evolution. (64)

———

I've had an awareness of the limitations of mortality since being diagnosed as a diabetic when I was 15 and want to ensure that I get to finish everything while I can. (52)

———

I've never said that I was against capitalism. What I've said is that people need to consume with more discretion. And I do commercial work for people that I respect and that I don't have an ethical conflict with. (46)

I define selling out as compromising your values just to make money. I think there are situations where working with a corporation demands compromises but there are others where it's possible to more or less have a corporation knowingly or unwittingly fund a creative project that allows you to maintain your integrity at the same time. (54)

———

Resonating is not selling out. Selling out is compromising your values to pander to the lowest common denominator. (16)

———

There are shitheads and good people in both the underground and the corporate world. Everything requires analysis. (52)

———

I really don't care about the concept of legitimacy from anyone else's perspective other than mine. (14)

———

Independence allows for personal expression, risk-taking, and rapid evolution that isn't possible on a more corporate or institutional scale. (54)

———

I'm not in politics, and I'm glad that that means I can speak my mind openly both verbally and through my art. (55)

———

People perceive that success has changed me. I'm still just as rebellious as I've always been but now I have more platforms at my disposal. (54)

———

As an artist, the more successful you become, the more people want to try to discredit your approach. (11)

———

I refuse to abandon nuance in my discussions
of politics to avoid the reductive false media
narratives. We should demand better
from the press. (55)

———

I think debate is really healthy. I think that the
most potent things are contentious. (63)

———

Any art about social issues or the environment
is political, whether or not it's interfacing
with candidates or being applied to a
specific election. (60)

———

Independence matters because homogeneity sucks. As we all know, bigger companies absorb smaller companies; systems become uniform, and things can become very monotonous and conformist. (54)

—

I've found that everything worth trying to get is maybe worth a little extra effort—versus just plugging into the grid. (62)

—

Art can break through predispositions by impacting people emotionally; then their intellectual side wants to justify their emotional response. (40)

The internet is a blessing and a curse because it democratizes things, but [this] also means that a lot of information and a lot of voices that have no credibility are just adding to the white noise. (66)

At the dawn of the internet, you could still have things out in the public that were provocative and mysterious, which is really impossible now. (44)

Social media creates echo chambers where people live very siloed lives. They hear what they want to hear. (61)

What I'm concerned about for the younger generation is a lot of distractions and overstimulation that maybe doesn't have much substance. That takes time away from taking a deep breath and looking at the best way to use their skill set and their philosophy in a way that's not about short-term gratification. (12)

———

There's something worthwhile in quality, not just quantity. The relationships that you form with other people, the time that you put into good literature or following politics—all of that should be on the mural level, not the meme level. (5)

———

Politicians understand how social media works, so they're communicating in a way that is repeating lies—then people repeat that on social media and things will not be vetted by more respected media. (61)

———

There's a difference between protecting free speech and protecting disinformation, misinformation, and conspiracy theories. Free speech is one thing, but it doesn't mean that you have to protect things that are false and harmful, and that's where the line needs to be drawn with the social media companies. (65)

———

Mark Zuckerberg and a bunch of other people have really hidden behind the idea of protecting free speech. It's been good for their business model, but it's not good for society. (65)

———

The problem is that the new media and new technology has this idea that "faster is better," but it's not better. It just means that people are scrambling to decode the misinformation and disinformation out there and wasting a lot of their time. (66)

———

My time is better spent producing art than policing the internet forums. (52)

———

I'm anti-violence, not anti-police, but I'm vehemently pro-justice. In my opinion, the activist groups are seeking justice and NEVER justifying violence. (59)

———

The widespread mistrust of the police stems from a pervasive unwillingness on the part of police to punish, or even acknowledge, bad behavior by police. (59)

———

Despite being polite, nonthreatening, and my infractions being nonviolent, most of my police encounters have been negative. That negativity ranges from simple sadistic disrespect for my basic humanity, like putting the handcuffs on excessively tight or refusing to provide a blanket in a freezing cold cell, to more serious sadism, like being beaten up or being banged around in the back of a cop car. (59)

———

The complete lack of regard for human life by the police that I've experienced firsthand is astonishing. (59)

———

The most despicable thing that has happened
to me four times while in jail is that the police
have refused to give me my insulin. I'm a type
one diabetic, and I will die without insulin,
yet even after many polite pleadings, the
police did nothing to administer my insulin.
I became so sick during two of my
longer stays in jail that I had to
be hospitalized. (59)

———

I only have one tattoo, and it reads "Diabetic" on my left bicep, a precaution insisted upon by my wife who knows that all tattoos are documented by the police during booking. In other words, my wife wanted the police to have to admit that they knew I was diabetic if I ever died in jail from not having my insulin.

(59)

If the police want to be trusted, they need to make moves to cut out their own cancer and demonstrate forward movement to minimize racial bias and unnecessary uses of violence.

(59)

I think any artist should focus on communicating the way they want through their art regardless of whether it will find favor with museums or galleries. (52)

———

The more you do your work, the more you develop and improve. (52)

———

I owe much of my success to a willingness to adapt to the square world's time frames and processes when needed. (54)

———

It can be challenging to have to develop and maintain your own systems, especially as a creative person when creativity is my strength and structure is my weakness. (54)

———

People do not like to be put on the spot about how to interpret things. And that's the failure of a lot of art to engage a broader audience, [because] people feel like they don't have the art credentials to interpret the work. (11)

———

At a lot of art shows, people are more worried about checking out the crowd than checking out the art. I can't really blame them when the art itself is less engaging than the written descriptions on the wall next to it. (3)

———

I think my understanding of what an icon was, what was iconic, and then how you developed a body of iconography, got a lot more sophisticated over the years. (72)

———

As art history books are produced, some of the things that are culturally relevant now may be overlooked, so a single piece of art may lose its importance. That's why it's important to judge the art in context. (52)

———

My art feels meaningless without the context of the street and its rich texture and unpredictability. (1)

———

When history judges my art, I hope it isn't by using one or two pieces. (52)

———

The most important thing is to be honest with yourself and be happy if you feel you've accomplished your vision—no matter what the rest of the world has to say. (14)

———

I live my life as a global citizen. (61)

———

I want diversity within the human population and beyond. (70)

———

The more people participate in the creation of culture, the richer the culture becomes. (62)

———

SOURCES

1. Fairey, Shepard. "Provocative Questions I.D. Magazine." *Obey Giant*, March 18, 2005. https://obeygiant.com /essays/provocative-questions/.

2. Fairey, Shepard. "Question: Education or Exploitation? Manufacturing Dissent." *Obey Giant*, March 18, 2004. https://obeygiant.com/essays/question-education-or -exploitation-manufacturing-dissent/.

3. Fairey, Shepard. "Heroes." *Obey Giant*, February 18, 2004. https://obeygiant.com/essays/heroes/.

4. Fairey, Shepard. "Sticker Art." *Obey Giant*, April 18, 2003. https://obeygiant.com/essays/sticker-art/.

5. Nechamkin, Sarah. "Shepard Fairey Thinks Streetwear Has Gotten as Silly as a Duct-Taped Banana." *Interview* magazine, December 29, 2019. https://www.interviewmagazine .com/artzshepard-fairey-street-art-obey-goldman-gallery -interview.

6. Aziz, Afdhel. "An Interview with Shepard Fairey: Artists Team Up with eBay to Design Bandanas to Support 'Get Out the Vote' Programs in the USA." Part 1 and part 2. *Forbes*, August 18, 2020. Part 1: https://www.forbes.com /sites/afdhelaziz/2020/08/18/an-interview-with

-shepherd-fairey-artists-team-up-with-ebay-to-design
-bandanas-to-support-get-out-the-vote-programs-in-the
-usa-pt1/?sh=696384a07075 and part 2: https://www
.forbes.com/sites/afdhelaziz/2020/08/18/an-interview
-with-shepherd-fairey-artists-team-up-with-ebay-to
-design-bandanas-to-support-get-out-the-vote-programs
-in-the-usa-pt2/?sh=4acaabc324d7.

7. Vitello, Gwynned. "Shepard Fairey: Punk and Progress."
Juxtapoz, February 7, 2024. https://www.juxtapoz.com
/news/magazine/features/from-the-magazine-shepard
-fairey-s-punk-and-progress/.

8. Fairey, Shepard. "Manufacturing Quality Dissent Since
1989." *Obey Giant*, 1990. https://obeygiant.com
/propaganda/manifesto/.

9. Fairey, Shepard. "From Obey Giant to Oceans, Artist
Shepard Fairey Reflects on His First Permanent Mural in
Boston." WBUR, July 27, 2021. https://www.wbur.org
/news/2021/07/23/shepard-faireys-new-england
-aquarium-right-whale.

10. Tay, Alison. "Interview: Shepard Fairey Talks Bringing His
Middle East–Inspired Work to Dubai." *Esquire Middle East*,
February 7, 2024. https://www.esquireme.com/culture
/interviews/51074-interview-shepard-fairey-talks
-bringing-his-middle-east-inspired-work-to-dubai.

11. Fairey, Shepard. "Oral History Interview with Shepard
Fairey, 2011 Feb. 10." Interview by Anne Louise Bayly

Berman. *Archives of American Art*, Smithsonian Institution. February 10, 2011. https://www.aaa.si.edu/download _pdf_transcript/ajax?record_id=edanmdm-AAADCD_oh _300233.

12. Williams-Kirtley, Gyasi. "The Philosopher's Dome: A Peek Inside the Mind of Shepard Fairey." *Highsnobiety*, February 7, 2024. https://www.highsnobiety.com/p/shepard-fairey -obey-interview/.

13. Helander, Bruce. "An Interview with Shepard Fairey." *Huffpost*, February 23, 2017. https://www.huffpost.com /entry/an-interview-with-shepard-fairey_b _58a9f605e4b0fa149f9ac7ac.

14. Brune, Adrian. "Shepard Fairey: 'My Goal Was to Make Art by Any Means Necessary.'[[thinspace]]" *The Guardian*, October 16, 2015. https://www.theguardian.com /artanddesign/2015/oct/16/shepard-fairey-my-goal-was -to-make-art-by-any-means-necessary.

15. O'Donoghue, Liam. "Interview: Shepard Fairey." *Mother Jones*, March/April, 2008. https://www.motherjones.com /politics/2008/03/interview-shepard-fairey/.

16. Simek, Peter. "Interview: Why Shepard Fairey Is Not a Sellout." D *Magazine*, February 7, 2012. https://www .dmagazine.com/arts-entertainment/2012/02 /interview-why-shepard-fairey-is-not-a-sellout/.

17. Fairey, Shepard. "An Interview with Shepard Fairey." *Obey Giant*, December 11, 2014. https://obeygiant.com/articles/an-interview-with-shepard-fairey/.

18. Fairey, Shepard. "Fairey Shepard Interview." *Art of the State*, November 2007. https://www.artofthestate.co.uk/london-street-art-2/shepard-fairey/shepard-fairey-interview/.

19. Donaldson, Eddie. "To Obey or Not to Obey: A Giant Question & An Artist's Mission." *Aware Now*, no. 23: 21–37. https://issuu.com/awarenessties/docs/awarenow_-_the_rightsedition/20?fr=sYzA3MTQ1MjA5MTg.

20. Bogojev, Sasha. "A Conversation with Shepard Fairey on 'Power and Equality.'" *Juxtapoz*, July 23, 2019. https://www.juxtapoz.com/news/street-art/a-conversation-with-shepard-fairey-on-power-and-equality/.

21. Kedmey, Karen. "Shepard Fairey on the Campaign Finance System's Role in Climate Change." *Artsy*, September 16, 2015. https://www.artsy.net/article/artsy-editorial-shepard-fairey-on-the-campaign-finance-system-s.

22. Mindich, Jessica. "Artist Shepard Fairey: Education & Precaution Can Help End Gun Violence." *Maria Shaver*, February 26, 2016. https://obeygiant.com/interview-education-precaution-can-help-end-gun-violence/.

23. Scrudato, Ken. "Six Questions about Art and Corruption with Shepard Fairey." *Black Book*, September 15, 2015. https://obeygiant.com/interview-with-blackbook-on-art-and-corruption/.

24. Moreno, Christian, and Craig Ibarra. "Rise and the Fall Fanzine Interview/Cover." *Rise and the Fall* 13, May/August 2009. https://obeygiant.com/rise-and-the-fall-fanzine -interviewcover/.

25. McVey, Kurt. "Shepard Fairey Paints It Black." *Interview* magazine. April 17, 2014. https://www.interviewmagazine .com/art/shepard-fairey-50-shades-of-black.

26. Wesson, Gail. "Idyllwild: Artist Shepard Fairey Shares Inspiration behind Work." *Press-Enterprise*, February 11, 2012. https://www.pressenterprise.com/2012/02/11 /idyllwild-artist-shepard-fairey-shares-inspiration-behind -work/.

27. Fairey, Shepard. OBEY GIANT: *Trailer (Official); A Hulu Original Documentary.* Hulu, November 7, 2017. Video, 1:50. https: //www.youtube.com/watch?v=IVvyI7BdYw8&t=82s.

28. Rogers, John. "Hope: Street Artist Shepard Fairey's Star Rises." *Colorado Daily,* July 30, 2009. https://www .coloradodaily.com/2009/07/30/hope-street-artist -shepard-faireys-star-rises/.

29. Booth, William. "Obama's On-the-Wall Endorsement." *Washington Post*, May 18, 2008. https://www .washingtonpost.com/wp-dyn/content/article/2008/05 /16/AR2008051601017.html.

30. Esaak, Shelley. "Shepard Fairey: The Controversial Street Artist." *Thought Co.*, August 27, 2018. https://www .thoughtco.com/shepard-fairey-quick-facts-183349.

31. Fairey, Shepard. "An Interview with Obey Creator Shepard Fairey." *Think Empire*, February 7, 2024. https://thinkempire.com/blogs/news/an-interview-with-obey-creator-shepard-fairey.

32. Ryzik, Melena. "Closer to Mainstream, Still a Bit Rebellious." *New York Times*, October 1, 2008. https://www.nytimes.com/2008/10/02/arts/design/02fair.html.

33. McVey, Kurt. "In His First New York Show in Five Years, Shepard Fairey Is Still Questioning Everything." *T: The New York Times Style Magazine*, August 20, 2015. https://www.nytimes.com/2015/08/20/t-magazine/shepard-fairey-on-our-hands-jacob-lewis.html?_r=0/.

34. Beer, Jeff. "Shepard Fairey: Obey Obama." *Creativity*, January 30, 2008. https://web.archive.org/web/20081216035557/http:/creativity-online.com/?action=news:article&newsId=124743&sectionId=behind_the_work.

35. Nelson, Joe Heaps. "Shepard Fairey: The Whitehot Interview." *Whitehot Magazine*, December 2010. https://whitehotmagazine.com/articles/2010-shepard-fairey-whitehot-interview/2172.

36. Fairey, Shepard. "Absoloot Sponsorship." In *OBEY: Supply & Demand; The Art of Shepard Fairey*, by Shepard Fairey, Roger Gastman, Steven Heller, Carlo McCormick, and Henry Rollins, 423–25. New York: Rizzoli, 2006.

37. Riefe, Jordan. "Why Shepard Fairey and PUSH Will Be Painting Outside Art of Elysium Gala." *Hollywood Reporter*, September 5, 2014. https://www.hollywoodreporter.com/news/general-news/why-shepard-fairey-push-will-730433/.

38. Fairey, Shepard. Introduction to *OBEY: Supply & Demand; The Art of Shepard Fairey*, i. By Shepard Fairey, Roger Gastman, Steven Heller, Carlo McCormick, and Henry Rollins. New York: Rizzoli, 2006.

39. Signore, John Del. "Shepard Fairey, Street Artist." *Gothamist*, June 21, 2007. https://web.archive.org/web/20090123172834/http:/gothamist.com/2007/06/21/interview_shepa.php.

40. Stosuy, Brandon. "Shepard Fairey on Political Art." *Creative Independent*, November 8, 2016. https://thecreativeindependent.com/people/shepard-fairey-on-political-art/.

41. Quotes provided by Shepard Fairey via email, August 20, 2022.

42. HB Team. "Shepard Fairey Explores Poignant Themes and Choices in 'The Future Is Unwritten.'" Interview by Aj Sacil. *Hypebeast*, September 29, 2023. https://hypebeast.com/2023/9/shepard-fairey-the-future-is-unwritten-singapore-solo-exhibition-interview.

43. Juca5056. "Obey's Shepard Fairey Has Only One Regret about His Obama 'HOPE' Poster." *Complex*, November 22,

2017. https://www.complex.com/pop-culture/a
/justin-caffier/shepard-fairey-obey-giant-interview.

44. Teicholz, Tom. "Shepard Fairey: Portrait of the Artist."
    Forbes, October 27, 2022. https://www.forbes.com/sites
    /tomteicholz/2022/10/27/
    shepard-fairey-portrait-of-the-artist/?sh=c9af9fb1dbe2.

45. Fairey, Shepard. "Spreading the Hope: Street Artist Shepard
    Fairey." Interview by Terry Gross. *Fresh Air*, NPR, January
    20, 2009. https://www.npr.org/transcripts/99466584.

46. Fairey, Shepard. "Shepard Fairey: Inspiration or Infringe-
    ment?" Interview by Terry Gross. *Fresh Air*, NPR, February
    26, 2009. https://www.npr.org/transcripts/101182453.

47. Aziz, Afdhel. "An Interview with Shepard Fairey: Artists
    Team Up with eBay to Design Bandanas to Support 'Get
    Out the Vote' Programs in the USA." Part 2. *Forbes*, August
    18, 2020. https://www.forbes.com/sites/afdhelaziz
    /2020/08/18/an-interview-with-shepherd-fairey
    -artists-team-up-with-ebay-to-design-bandanas-to
    -support-get-out-the-vote-programs-in-the-usa-pt2/?sh
    =40594d7e24d7.

48. "Shepard Fairey Talks Us through 5 Prints from His Career
    (Now for Sale on Artnet Auctions)." *Artnet Auctions*, March
    15, 2023. https://news.artnet.com/art-world/shepard
    -fairey-art-as-activism-2268931.

49. Yu, Tim. "Nineteeneightyfouria: Shepard Fairey Interview." *Cool Hunting*, October 12, 2007. https://coolhunting.com/culture/nineteeneightyf/.

50. Rauch, Dan "Plasma." "Dan 'Plasma' Rauch: The Phenomenology of Shepard Fairey." *Widewalls*, June 1, 2022. https://www.widewalls.ch/magazine/dan-rauch-shepard-fairey-interview.

51. Hogarth, Vicki. "Profile: Shepard Fairey." *View the Vibe*, November 4, 2014. https://viewthevibe.com/shepard-fairey-interview/.

52. "Shepard Fairey." In *Beyond the Street: The 100 Leading Figures in Urban Art*, edited by Patrick Nguyen and Stuart Mackenzie, 378–83. Berlin: Gestalten, 2010. https://archive.org/details/beyondstreet100l0000unse/page/378/mode/2up.

53. Xavier, Jeremy. "Andre Is Everything and Andre Is Nothing." *Loud Paper* 3, no. 3. http://www.loudpapermag.com/articles/andre-is-everything-and-andre-is-nothing-shepard-fairey.

54. Traynor, Cian. "How Shepard Fairey Survives as a Subversive Street Artist." *Huck*, August 6, 2016. https://www.huckmag.com/article/heroes-of-independence-shepard-fairey-success.

55. Fairey, Shepard. Email to Bradley R. Carlson. *Obey Giant*, June 16, 2015. https://obeygiant.com/giving-up-on-president-obama/.

56. Fairey, Shepard. "Shepard Fairey Talks Music and Art." *Obey Giant*, September 22, 2015. https://obeygiant.com /shepard-fairey-talks-music-and-art/.

57. Stein, Chris, and Shepard Fairey. "Shepard in Conversation with Chris Stein via Neuehouse." *NeueJournal*, September 24, 2015. https://obeygiant.com/shepard-in-conversation -with-chris-stein-via-neuehouse/.

58. Armand, Dan. "Shepard Fairey Talks Sharpening His Focus & Solo Exhibition." Interview by Pietro Truba. *1xRun*. https://news.1xrun.com/shepard-fairey-talks-sharpening -his-focus-solo-exhibition/.

59. Fairey, Shepard. "Violence and Discourse." *Obey Giant*, July 11, 2016. https://obeygiant.com/violence-and -discourse/.

60. Brooks, Katherine. "'Hope' Artist Shepard Fairey Explains Why He's Voting for Hillary Clinton." *Huffpost*, August 15, 2016. https://www.huffpost.com/entry/hope-artist -shepard-fairey-new-art_n_57adf886e4b071840411043a.

61. Carvalho, Catarina. "Obey: 'If you don't like vulnerable people harmed by gentrification, vote for politicians that protect vulnerable people!'" *Mensagem de Lisboa*, July 22, 2023. https://amensagem.pt/2023/07/22/ shepard-fairey-gentrification-underdogs-vhils/.

62. Pop, Iggy. "Shepard Fairey." *Interview* magazine, April 27, 2010. https://www.interviewmagazine.com/art/shepard -fairey.

63. Rojo, Jaime, and Steven Harrington. "Shepard Fairey: Too 'Street' for Corporate, Too Corporate for the Street." *Huffpost*, July 4, 2011. https://www.huffpost.com/entry /post_b_887498.

64. "On the Cover: Shepard Fairey." *Delayed Gratification*, October 9, 2015. https://www.slow-journalism.com /delayed-gratification-magazine/on-the-cover-shepard -fairey.

65. Webb, Marcus. "Shepard Fairey on Free Speech, Trump, Truth—and Ten Years of Delayed Gratification." *Delayed Gratification*, November 30, 2020. https://www.slow -journalism.com/long-reads/shepard-fairey-on-free -speech-trump-truth-and-ten-years-of-delayed -gratification.

66. Fairey, Shepard. "Freedom of the Press." *Delayed Gratification*, no. 1 (2010). https://www.slow-journalism.com/back -issue/test-item-04.

67. Franklin, Oliver. "Shepard Fairey on What Barack Obama's 'Hope' Poster Would Say in 2012 and Redesigning the Rolling Stones." *GQ*, October 30, 2012. https://obeygiant .com/gq-online-shepard-fairey-on-what-barack-obamas -hope-poster-would-say-in-2012-and-redesigning-the -rolling-stones/.

68. "Interview with Shepard Fairey." *Sex Sells Magazine*, December 18, 1997. https://obeygiant.com/articles/sex -sells-magazine/.

69. Reaves, Wendy Rick. "Artist Interview: Shepard Fairey." Interview recorded at the National Portrait Gallery, July 7, 2009. Transcript available at Smithsonian Digital Volunteers: Transcription Center. https://transcription.si.edu/mediaPlayer/sound/43147.

70. Fairey, Shepard. "How Can Street Art Change the World?" Channel 4 News, October 23, 2019. Video, 42:17. https://www.youtube.com/watch?v=c8wEMkfPHzg.

71. Fairey, Shepard. Interview by Jared Leto. *Beyond the Horizon*, season 2. February 5, 2020. Video, 6:13. https://www.youtube.com/watch?v=jZprBOhuHZ8.

72. Pricco, Evan. "Shepard Fairey: The Iconic Icon." *Juxtapoz*, Winter 2024 Quarterly. https://www.juxtapoz.com/news/magazine/features/shepard-fairey-the-iconic-icon/.

73. Baltin, Steve. "Q&A: Shepard Fairey on Why He Lent His Talents to Playing for Change Foundation—Music and Education." *Forbes*, September 8, 2022. https://www.forbes.com/sites/stevebaltin/2022/09/08/qa-shepard-fairey-on-why-he-lent-his-talents-to-playing-for-change-foundation---music-and-education/?sh=50b92c83781e.

74. Fairey, Shepard. "Shepard Fairey on Barbara Kruger." *Juxtapoz*, no. 118 (2010). https://hypebeast.com/2010/11/juxtapoz-shepard-fairey-on-barbara-kruger.

75. Eller, Matthew. "Artist Interview: Shepard Fairey." *Street Art News*, September 29, 2023. https://streetartnews.net/2023/09/__trashed.html.

76. Heller, Steven. "Still Obeying after All These Years." In OBEY: *Supply & Demand; The Art of Shepard Fairey*, by Shepard Fairey, Roger Gastman, Steven Heller, Carlo McCormick, and Henry Rollins, 93–101. New York: Rizzoli, 2006.

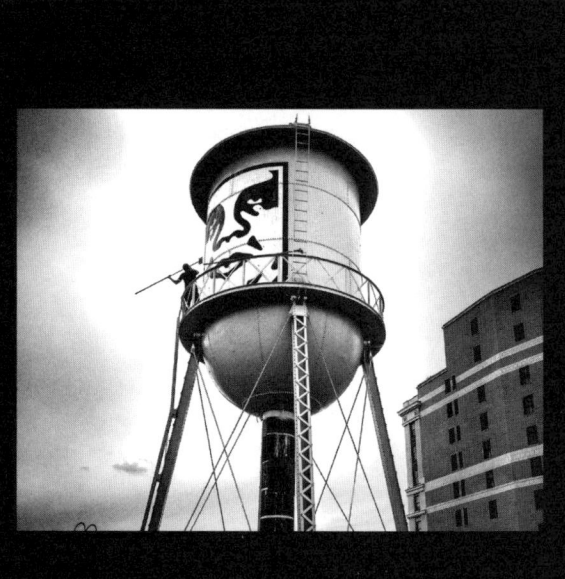

CHRONOLOGY

1970

Shepard Fairey is born on February 15 in Charleston,
South Carolina. His father, Strait Fairey, is a doctor,
and his mother, Charlotte, is a realtor.

1984

Fairey buys his first skateboard.

1988

He graduates from Idyllwild Arts Academy in Idyll-
wild, California, which he had transferred to from
Porter-Gaud School, a college preparatory school in
Charleston.

1989

Fairey creates the "Andre the Giant Has a Posse"
sticker, which he refers to as "a spontaneous, happy
accident."

1990

He develops the OBEY GIANT art campaign on the streets.

1990

He takes over a Buddy Cianci campaign billboard in Providence, Rhode Island, replacing Cianci's face and name with that of Andre the Giant.

1992

Fairey graduates from the Rhode Island School of Design with a Bachelor of Fine Arts in Illustration.

1994

Fairey's work is included in *Minimal Trix*, a group exhibition curated by Aaron Rose, at the Alleged Gallery, the Museum of Contemporary Art, and the Cooper Hewitt Design Museum, all in New York City, respectively. *Minimal Trix* is a major stepping stone for the participating artists.

1995

Fairey cofounds *Subliminal*, a skateboard brand focusing on artists, with skateboarder Blaize Blouin.

Fairey's work is shown at the Holly Solomon Gallery in New York City.

1996

Fairey moves from Providence, Rhode Island, to San Diego, California.

1998

Fairey's work is shown in New York City and Kansas City, Missouri.

1999

Fairey's work is included in the Tokion Neo Graffiti Project in San Francisco and is shown in numerous exhibitions internationally.

2000

Fairey forms OBEY Clothing.

2001

He moves to Los Angeles from San Diego.

2002

Fairey's work is shown in numerous solo and group
exhibitions across the United States and in London
and Tokyo.

2003

Fairey founds the creative agency Studio Number One in
Los Angeles with his wife, Amanda.

He becomes a member of and contributor to, the Los
Angeles County Museum of Art (LACMA) Graphic
Arts Council.

His work is shown in numerous solo group exhibitions
internationally, including in Berlin, Germany; Paris,
France; and Sydney, Australia.

2004

Fairey creates *Swindle* magazine with Roger Gastman.

2005

Fairey participates in an artist residency for the Contemporary Museum in Honolulu, Hawaii.

His work is shown in twenty-nine group and solo exhibitions internationally.

2006

OBEY: *Supply & Demand; The Art of Shepard Fairey* is published.

2007

OBEY Awareness, a philanthropic program through OBEY Clothing, is born to support social responsibility through partnerships.

French designer agnès B. stages a project between Fairey and graffiti artist WK Interact, which takes place in both Paris and Tokyo.

Three notable solo exhibitions, *E Pluribus Venom*, *Nineteeneightyfouria*, and *Imperfect Union*, open in New York City, London, and Los Angeles, respectively.

2008

Fairey creates the Obama "Hope" poster as a guerrilla campaign for then-presidential candidate Barack Obama.

Beautiful Losers, a documentary featuring Fairey and several other "DIY" artists from the skateboarding and graffiti communities, premieres at the South by Southwest (SXSW) festival in Austin, Texas.

Fairey participates in the group exhibition *Regime Change Starts at Home* with artists Al Farrow and Paul D. Miller (DJ Spooky) at Irvine Contemporary in Washington, DC.

Duality of Humanity, a solo exhibition, opens at White Walls Gallery in San Francisco.

2009

Supply and Demand: 20 Year Survey, Fairey's first major solo exhibition, debuts at the Institute of Contemporary Art (ICA) in Boston, Massachusetts, and travels to the Warhol Museum in Pittsburgh, Pennsylvania, and the Contemporary Arts Center (CAC) in Cincinnati, Ohio.

2010

May Day, a solo exhibition featuring works of portraiture of political activists, artists, and musicians, opens at Deitch Projects in New York City.

Printed Matters, a solo exhibition focused on Fairey's printed works, opens at Subliminal Projects in Los Angeles. The exhibition is the first in a continuous series of exhibitions in multiple locations, all focusing on printed material.

Fairey receives the Orchids & Onions Award.

2011

Your Ad Here, a solo exhibition, opens in Copenhagen, Denmark.

2012

Harmony and Discord, a solo exhibition at Pace Prints, opens in New York City.

Fairey collaborates with Neil Young to design the art for his album *Americana*, which reinterprets classic American folk songs.

Sound and Vision, a solo exhibition inspired by Fairey's love of music, opens at StolenSpace Gallery in London.

Printed Matters opens in Dallas, Texas.

2013

Sid: Superman Is Dead, a collaborative exhibition between Fairey and photographer Dennis Morris, opens at Subliminal Projects.

2014

Shepard Fairey: 50 Shades of Black, a solo exhibition of album cover artwork, opens at Subliminal Projects.

Power and Glory, an exhibition of Fairey's artwork alongside that of Jasper Johns, opens at the Halsey Institute in Fairey's hometown, Charleston.

Fairey receives the Tony Goldman Visionary Artist Award.

2015

Your Eyes Here, a retrospective of Fairey's artwork, opens in Málaga, Spain.

Shepard Fairey: On Our Hands, opens at the Jacob Lewis Gallery in New York City.

Fairey receives an honorary doctorate from the Pratt
Institute in Brooklyn.

A climate crisis–themed artwork by Fairey is installed at
the Eiffel Tower to coincide with the COP21 Climate
Conference in Paris.

Printed Matters & Public Matter opens in Detroit.

2016

Earth Crisis, an exhibition in conjunction with Fairey's
Eiffel Tower installation, opens at Galerie Itinerrance
in Paris.

Fairey collaborates with the estate of photographer Jim
Marshall to reinterpret some of Marshall's iconic
photographs for the exhibition *American Civics* in San
Francisco.

Visual Disobedience, a retrospective of Fairey's work accom-
panied by several large-scale public murals, opens in
Hong Kong.

2017

Fairey creates the art series *We the People* for the global
Women's Marches.

OBEY GIANT: The Art and Dissent of Shepard Fairey, a documentary by Hulu, is released.

Fairey receives numerous awards, including the P.S. ARTS heART Award, the Muslim Public Affairs Council (MPAC) Voices of Courage Media Award, and the Art Wynwood Tony Goldman Lifetime Artistic Achievement Award.

Printed Matters opens in Sydney, Australia; Lisbon, Portugal; and Seattle, Washington.

Damaged, a major solo exhibition, opens at the Library Street Collective in Los Angeles.

2018

Fairey and his team paint a large-scale mural at the Vienna International Airport in Vienna, Austria, in conjunction with the exhibition *Golden Future* at Galerie Ernst Hilger.

Salad Days, a solo exhibition on the theme of Fairey's early punk influences, opens at the Cranbrook Art Museum in Bloomfield Hills, Michigan.

Fairey and his team paint *Ideal Power*, a large-scale mural, in Aspen, Colorado.

Fairey participates in *Beyond the Streets*, a major group exhibition in Los Angeles, featuring many top graffiti and street artists.

Force Majeure, a major solo exhibition, opens at the Moscow Museum of Modern Art (MMOMA) in Moscow, Russia.

2019

Beyond the Streets travels to Brooklyn, New York.

Facing the Giant—Three Decades of Dissent: Shepard Fairey, a solo exhibition, marks thirty years since OBEY GIANT was created. The exhibition travels internationally.

Fairey receives the Cesar Chavez Legacy Awards Honoree.

2020

Fairey's work is included in *Sidewalk Activism*, a group exhibition featuring street and graffiti artists, in Oceanside, California.

2021

Future Mosaic, a major solo exhibition, opens at the Opera
    Gallery in Dubai, United Arab Emirates.
Fairey receives an Honorary Doctorate of Fine Arts from
    the Rhode Island School of Design.

2022

Printed Matters: Paix et Justice opens in Montreal, Quebec.
Multiple solo exhibitions, including *Eyes Open Minds
    Open*, *Backward Forward*, and *New Clear Power*, open in
    Seoul, Korea; Dallas, Texas; and Munich, Germany,
    respectively.

2023

Beyond the Streets travels to London.
Heavy Metal, an exhibition of works on metal, opens in
    Denver, Colorado.
Printed Matters: While Supplies Last, an exhibition address-
    ing environmental and social challenges, opens in
    Portugal.

Fairey participates in *Urban(R)evolution*, a group
    exhibition, in Portugal.
Printed Matters: Raise the Level opens at the STRAAT
    Museum in Amsterdam, and Fairey and his team
    paint a mural on the side wall of the museum.
Shepard Fairey: Icons, a solo exhibition, opens at
    Subliminal Projects.

ACKNOWLEDGMENTS

First, I extend my deepest gratitude to Shepard Fairey, whose profound insights, inspiring words, and remarkable artistic vision provided the foundation for this publication. Your commitment to social justice, activism, and creativity continues to empower us all.

My utmost appreciation goes as well to Amanda Fairey, whose support and ceaseless inspiration made this book a possibility.

I would also like to extend my deepest thanks to Victoria Yarnish, Dan Flores, Angel Enciso, Jon Furlong, Vanthi Nguyen, Ajani Purnell, and the entire studio team for their dedication and expertise, which have helped shape and refine this project.

My thanks as well to Carlo McCormick for his exceptional insights and unique perspectives on Shepard and many other artists.

My sincere appreciation, as always, to the entire team at Princeton University Press, especially Michelle Komie, Christie Henry, Terri O'Prey, Cathy Slovensky, Jacqueline Poirier,

Colleen Suljic, Laurie Schlesinger, Cathy Felgar, Jodi Price, Kathryn Stevens, Annie Miller, William Skurka, and Alexandria Leonard. We remain extremely grateful to PUP for their continued professionalism, encouragement, and passion for our projects together throughout the years.

I would also like to extend my thanks to Mike Dean, whose friendship and invaluable insights into the world of music are deeply appreciated.

Very special thanks to Fiona Graham for her invaluable research and organization of this project, and of the ISMs series as a whole. My thanks as well to Susan Delson for her insightful editorial assistance, and to Katy Kiefer and Matthew Christensen for their research support.

My sincere thanks as well to Karen Lautanen for her organizational aid on this project and many others, and to Taliesin Thomas and Steven Rodríguez for their continued support.

Finally, I give all my bottomless gratitude to my amazing wife, Abbey, and to my wonderful children, Justin, Ethan, Ellie, and Jonah, for their love and encouragement.

As always, I give endless love and thanks to my mother, Judith.

LARRY WARSH

Shepard Fairey is a contemporary street artist, graphic designer, and activist, and the founder of OBEY Clothing and the creative agency Studio Number One. In 1989, while at Rhode Island School of Design studying for his Bachelor of Fine Arts in Illustration, Fairey created the "Andre the Giant Has a Posse" sticker, which later evolved into the OBEY GIANT art campaign. In 2008, his portrait of then Democratic candidate Barack Obama became an internationally recognized emblem of hope. He is known for the "We the People" campaign debuted during the 2017 Women's Marches worldwide. Fairey has painted more than 135 public murals and has become one of the most sought-after and provocative artists globally, changing the way people converse about art and view the urban landscape.

Larry Warsh has been active in the art world for more than thirty years as a publisher and artist-collaborator. An early collector of Keith Haring and Jean-Michel Basquiat, Warsh was a lead organizer for the exhibition *Basquiat: The Unknown Notebooks*, which debuted at the Brooklyn Museum, New York, in 2015, and later traveled to several American museums. He has loaned artworks by Haring and Basquiat from his collection to numerous exhibitions worldwide, and he served as a curatorial consultant on *Keith Haring | Jean-Michel Basquiat: Crossing Lines* for the National Gallery of Victoria. The founder of *Museums Magazine*, Warsh has been involved in many publishing projects and is the editor of the ISMs series and several other titles published by Princeton University Press, including Jean-Michel Basquiat's *The Notebooks* (2017), *Keith Haring: 31 Subway Drawings* (2021), and two books by Ai Weiwei, *Humanity* (2018) and *Weiwei-isms* (2012). Warsh has served on the board of the Getty Museum Photographs Council and was a founding member of the Basquiat Authentication Committee until its dissolution in 2012.

ILLUSTRATIONS

Frontispiece: Portrait of Shepard Fairey. Photograph by Jeffrey Rovner.

Page 136: Shepard Fairey, Courtesy of the artist, obeygiant.com. Photograph by Jon Furlong.

ISMs

Larry Warsh, Series Editor

The ISMs series distills the voices of an exciting range of visual artists and designers into captivating, beautifully made books of quotations for a new generation of readers. In turn passionate, inspiring, humorous, witty, and challenging, these collections offer powerful statements on topics ranging from contemporary culture, politics, and race, to creativity, humanity, and the role of art in the world. Books in this series are edited by Larry Warsh and published by Princeton University Press in association with No More Rulers.

Minter-isms, Marilyn Minter

Fairey-isms, Shepard Fairey

Abramović-isms, Marina Abramović

JR-isms, JR

Holzer-isms: Artist's Edition, Jenny Holzer

Neshat-isms, Shirin Neshat

Judy Chicago-isms, Judy Chicago

Pharrell-isms, Pharrell Williams

Hirst-isms, Damien Hirst

Warhol-isms, Andy Warhol

Arsham-isms, Daniel Arsham

Abloh-isms, Virgil Abloh

Futura-isms, Futura

Haring-isms, Keith Haring

Basquiat-isms, Jean-Michel Basquiat